ABDO
Publishing Company

Manage Feelings

Buddy BOOKS
Get Healthy

A Buddy Book by Sarah Tieck

VISIT US AT
www.abdopublishing.com

Published by ABDO Publishing Company, PO Box 398166, Minneapolis, MN 55439.

Printed in the United States of America, North Mankato, Minnesota.
102011
012012

 PRINTED ON RECYCLED PAPER

Coordinating Series Editor: Rochelle Baltzer
Contributing Editors: Megan M. Gunderson, BreAnn Rumsch, Marcia Zappa
Graphic Design: Jenny Christensen
Cover Photograph: *iStockphoto*: ©iStockphoto.com/Blue_Cutler.
Interior Photographs/Illustrations: *Eighth Street Studio* (p. 26); *iStockphoto*: ©iStockphoto.com/aabejon (p. 5), ©iStockphoto.com/Aaron-H (p. 13), ©iStockphoto.com/AmpH (p. 29), ©iStockphoto.com/digitalskillet (p. 25), ©iStockphoto.com/Elenathewise (p. 15), ©iStockphoto.com/goodynewshoes (p. 26), ©iStockphoto.com/lisafx (pp. 11, 27), ©iStockphoto.com/nicolesy (p. 27), ©iStockphoto.com/princessdlaf (p. 21), ©iStockphoto.com/Syldavia (p. 19), ©iStockphoto.com/YinYang (p. 29); *Photo Researchers, Inc.*: John Bavosi (p. 19); *Photolibrary*: Age fotostock (p. 23); *Shutterstock*: Blend Images (p. 17), Hung Chung Chih (p. 30), olly (p. 7), Supri Suharjoto (p. 21), Christophe Testi (p. 5), Guido Vrola (p. 9), wavebreakmedia ltd (p. 5), Zurijeta (p. 7).

Library of Congress Cataloging-in-Publication Data

Tieck, Sarah, 1976-
  Manage feelings / Sarah Tieck.
    p. cm. -- (Get healthy)
  ISBN 978-1-61783-235-2
  1. Emotions--Juvenile literature. I. Title.
  BF531.T54 2012
  152.4--dc23
                          2011034604

Table of Contents

Healthy Living

Your body is amazing! It does thousands of things each day. It lets you joke, run, and laugh. A healthy body helps you feel good and live well!

In order to be healthy, you must take care of your body. Managing your feelings helps your body stay well. So, let's learn more about your **emotions**!

Your many different emotions help you learn about yourself.

Feelings 101

Everyone has **emotions**. You've probably felt shy, sad, scared, and happy. Sometimes, your emotions feel very strong.

Emotions are caused by thoughts and events. So, they can change quickly. You may even feel more than one at the same time!

When something makes you feel sad, you may cry.

If something makes you feel mad, you may yell or stomp your feet.

More Than a Feeling

When a thought or event happens, your brain lets out **chemicals**. These cause your body to act.

Often, your body acts before you are aware of what is happening. So, pay attention to your feelings. This can help you get in better control of how you behave.

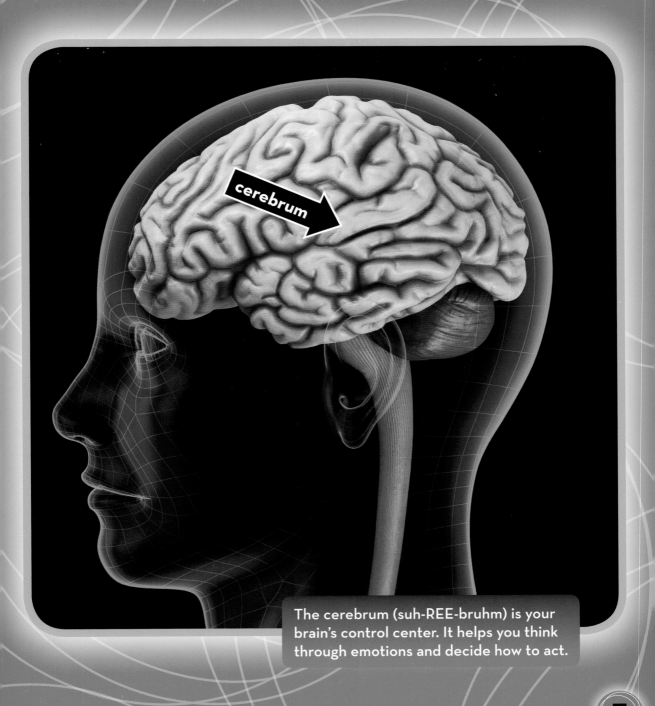

cerebrum

The cerebrum (suh-REE-bruhm) is your brain's control center. It helps you think through emotions and decide how to act.

Mad, Mad World

What do you do when you get in trouble or someone yells at you? Do your **muscles** tighten? Do you yell or stomp your feet? Maybe you even feel like you want to hit someone or something.

Everyone feels angry at times. But if you act without thinking, you can hurt someone's body or feelings. You might not be able to stop anger. But, you can control how you behave.

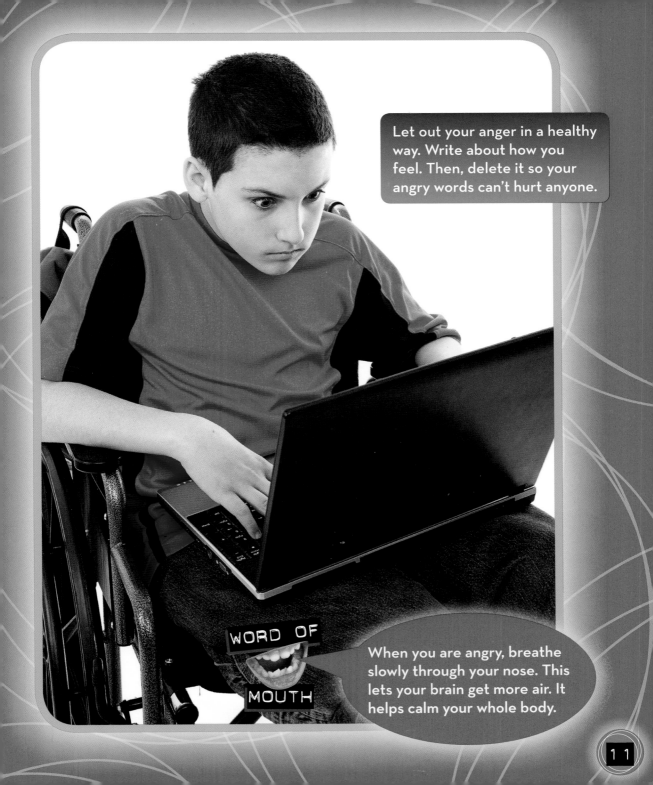

Let out your anger in a healthy way. Write about how you feel. Then, delete it so your angry words can't hurt anyone.

WORD OF MOUTH

When you are angry, breathe slowly through your nose. This lets your brain get more air. It helps calm your whole body.

To control your actions, pay attention to how your body feels. Also, name your feelings. When you notice a strong feeling, such as anger, take a few minutes by yourself.

There are ways to keep calm when you feel angry. Take a walk, listen to music, or hit a pillow. When you are in control again, you can better decide what to do.

WORD OF MOUTH

When you are mad, try starting your sentences with "I" instead of "you." Explain how you feel instead of blaming someone else.

When you feel angry, close your eyes and count to ten before you say or do anything.

13

Feeling Down

If a friend moves away, you may feel sad. When you are sad, you might cry or feel like spending time alone.

Feeling sad is normal. Crying or talking to a friend can be good for your body. This lets out your feelings.

WORD OF MOUTH

Do you ever feel sad? Some people call this having the blues.

When you let out your feelings, your whole body feels calmer.

If someone you love dies or your pet is lost, you may feel very sad. This is called grief. It may take a long time to heal from a loss. Your body might feel extra tired.

Some people suffer from depression. Depression is a type of sadness that lasts a long time. It is a serious condition that can cause other health problems. Many people who suffer from depression need help from a doctor.

People who have depression may take medicine to help them manage their sad feelings.

WORD OF MOUTH

Remember people who are gone by looking at pictures. This will remind you of happy times you shared.

Fight or Flight

How do you feel after you hear a loud noise? Does your heart race? Maybe you even scream.

When you feel afraid, a part of your brain called the amygdala acts quickly. It alerts the hypothalamus, which causes body changes.

Your **muscles** may feel tight, or your heart may beat fast. Your brain decides if you need to run away or **defend** yourself. This is called the fight-or-flight response.

How It Sounds

amygdala (uh-MIHG-duh-luh)
hypothalamus (heye-poh-THA-luh-muhs)

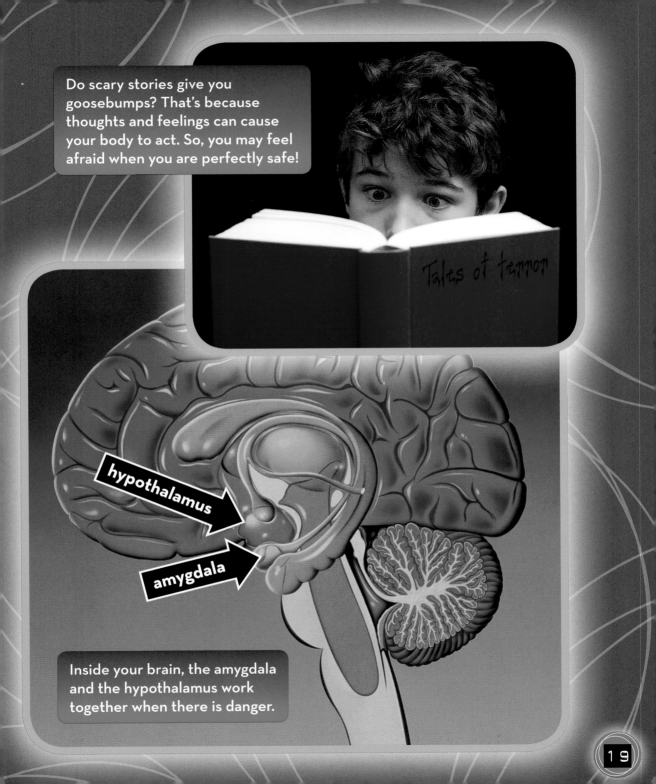

Do scary stories give you goosebumps? That's because thoughts and feelings can cause your body to act. So, you may feel afraid when you are perfectly safe!

Tales of Terror

hypothalamus

amygdala

Inside your brain, the amygdala and the hypothalamus work together when there is danger.

You might not be able to stop fearful feelings. But you can learn to manage your thoughts. Some thoughts are true, but others are not. Changing an untrue fearful thought into a positive one will help you feel more in control.

Knowing how to keep yourself safe will also help you feel less afraid. If you are scared of a house fire, know your family's safety plan in case of one. That way, you will feel prepared and in control.

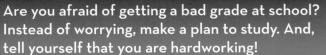
Are you afraid of getting a bad grade at school? Instead of worrying, make a plan to study. And, tell yourself that you are hardworking!

Are you afraid to go to sleep at night? Remind yourself that you are safe. And, talk to an adult about your fears.

Now and Later

Emotions affect your body. Over time, negative feelings can lead to health problems. For example, you can get sick more easily if you feel **stressed**. So, learning to manage your feelings helps your body stay well.

When you cry, your tears let out chemicals. This can help calm your body.

It is important to manage your feelings. If you are upset or worried, talk to an adult. This can make you feel better. An adult can get a doctor to help, too.

Holding in your feelings is not healthy. It can cause you to have an upset stomach, pain, trouble sleeping, or more serious health problems. Make good choices now to keep your body healthy for many years!

People can help each other by talking and listening.

25

Brain Food

Are all fears the same?

All fears may feel real, but some are not. Sometimes, people feel scared about things that could happen. This type of worry is called anxiety (ang-ZEYE-uh-tee). It can make your body feel as if something scary is really happening.

Why do I feel better when I laugh?

Laughing lets out **chemicals** that help you feel happy. Activities such as walking and playing outside also help your body let out these chemicals.

What is therapy?

When people need help managing their feelings, they may see special doctors. These doctors ask questions about how people feel. Then, they listen and teach skills for managing feelings.

Making Healthy Choices

Remember that managing your feelings keeps your body well. Work to recognize your thoughts and **emotions**. This will help you control your actions.

Managing feelings is just one part of a healthy life. Each positive choice you make will help you stay healthy!

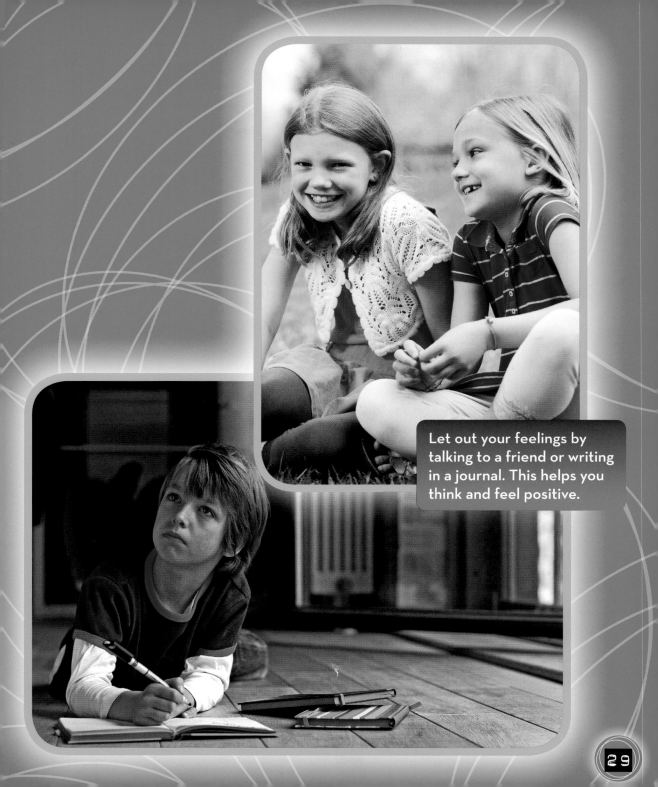

Let out your feelings by talking to a friend or writing in a journal. This helps you think and feel positive.

BODY POWER

✔ Some people gain or lose weight from **stress**. So, manage your stress to help keep your body at a healthy weight.

✔ Are you worried about something? Tell a joke or watch a silly movie to relax.

SAD SACK

✔ Not getting enough sleep can make you feel sad or stressed. Make sure you are sleeping well!

✔ Darkness causes some people to feel sad. If you are feeling blue, take a walk in the sunshine.

BUST STRESS

✔ Exercise helps reduce stress. After a long walk or run, your body lets out **chemicals** that make you feel good.

Important Words

chemical (KEH-mih-kuhl) a substance that can cause reactions and changes.

defend to fight danger in order to keep safe.

emotion (ih-MOH-shuhn) a state of mind or feeling.

muscle (MUH-suhl) body tissue, or layers of cells, that helps move the body.

stress a feeling of worry that may lead to some illnesses.

Web Sites

To learn more about managing feelings, visit ABDO Publishing Company online. Web sites about managing feelings are featured on our Book Links page. These links are routinely monitored and updated to provide the most current information available.

www.abdopublishing.com

Index